PRINCEWILL LAGANG

Guardians of Wealth: The Julia Flesher Koch Legacy

First published by PRINCEWILL LAGANG 2023

Copyright © 2023 by Princewill Lagang

All rights reserved. No part of this publication may be reproduced, stored or transmitted in any form or by any means, electronic, mechanical, photocopying, recording, scanning, or otherwise without written permission from the publisher. It is illegal to copy this book, post it to a website, or distribute it by any other means without permission.

Princewill Lagang asserts the moral right to be identified as the author of this work.

First edition

This book was professionally typeset on Reedsy.
Find out more at reedsy.com

Contents

1	Introduction - The Tapestry of Wealth and Legacy	1
2	Inheritance and Ambition	3
3	Foundations of Fortune	5
4	Shifting Tides: Challenges and Transformations	7
5	The Phoenix Rises: Reinvention and Resilience	9
6	Legacy in Flux: Navigating Generational Shifts	11
7	Crossroads of Influence: The Koch Legacy in the 21st Century	13
8	Echoes of the Past, Visions of the Future	15
9	The Legacy Unfolds: Charting New Horizons	17
10	Reckoning and Renewal: The Legacy's Epiphany	20
11	Beyond Boundaries: A Legacy in Full Bloom	23
12	Reflections and Continuity: The Legacy Lives On	26
13	Epilogue: A Lasting Legacy	29
14	Summary	31

1

Introduction - The Tapestry of Wealth and Legacy

In the annals of American business history, the Koch family stands as a formidable force, weaving a tapestry of wealth, influence, and societal impact. "Guardians of Wealth: The Julia Flesher Koch Legacy" invites readers into the intricate world of one of the nation's most influential families, exploring the multifaceted journey that spans generations and industries.

As we embark on this narrative journey, the spotlight falls on Julia Flesher Koch, the matriarch who steered the family legacy through the currents of change. From the modest roots of Koch Industries to its evolution into a global conglomerate, the Koch family's story reflects not only the triumphs of American entrepreneurship but also the complexities and responsibilities that come with immense wealth.

The narrative unfolds against the backdrop of a changing America, navigating the family's ascent through post-World War II industrial landscapes, economic upheavals, and societal transformations. Readers will be immersed in the family's business ventures, witnessing the strategic decisions, challenges, and innovations that define their legacy.

But this is not merely a story of business success; it's a tale of familial bonds, generational transitions, and the delicate dance between tradition and progress. Julia Flesher Koch emerges as a central figure, not just as a guardian of wealth but as a steward of values, ethics, and a commitment to shaping a positive impact on the world.

The narrative is a journey through the corridors of power, exploring the family's engagements with politics, philanthropy, and societal narratives. As the legacy evolves, readers will witness the family grappling with societal reckonings, adapting to changing times, and contemplating the responsibilities that come with vast financial influence.

"Guardians of Wealth" invites readers to ponder the broader implications of immense wealth, its role in shaping the course of history, and the responsibilities borne by those who hold its reins. As we delve into the chapters that follow, we unravel not just the story of a family but a reflection on the complexities of wealth, the endurance of values, and the ongoing saga of the Guardians of Wealth.

2

Inheritance and Ambition

The morning sun cast a warm glow over the bustling city of Wichita, Kansas, as Julia Flesher Koch awoke to a new chapter in her life. The legacy of the Koch family, a name synonymous with wealth and influence, had woven itself into the fabric of American business. As Julia rose from her elegant bed, she couldn't escape the weight of the responsibility that came with being a guardian of this vast financial empire.

The Koch family had its origins in the mid-20th century, when Fred C. Koch, a chemical engineer, founded what would become Koch Industries. His vision and entrepreneurial spirit set the stage for a multi-generational saga of wealth creation and power. Now, as Julia stepped into the role of matriarch, she felt the weight of not just the family fortune but the expectations and legacies of those who came before her.

In this first chapter, we delve into the roots of the Koch dynasty, exploring the entrepreneurial spirit that fueled its rise. Fred C. Koch's journey from building refineries to establishing a conglomerate that touched various industries laid the foundation for the immense wealth that would follow. The narrative weaves through the challenges faced by the family patriarch, the triumphs that shaped the Koch Industries, and the values instilled in subsequent generations.

Julia's entrance into this world of opulence and influence was marked by her marriage to David Koch, one of the four Koch brothers. As she navigated the complexities of being a Koch, she found herself at the intersection of privilege and responsibility. The chapter explores the dynamics of the Koch family, the relationships that bound them, and the values that shaped their approach to business and philanthropy.

As we peer into Julia's early years within the Koch family, we unravel the layers of her character – her aspirations, her passions, and the challenges she faced in balancing the demands of her personal and public life. The narrative unfolds against the backdrop of a changing America, where wealth and power intersect with social and political landscapes.

The chapter concludes with a glimpse into the present, where Julia stands as the torchbearer of the Koch legacy. Her journey, like that of the family, is one of evolution and adaptation. The stage is set for a compelling exploration of the guardianship of wealth and the responsibility that comes with shaping the destiny of one of America's most influential families.

3

Foundations of Fortune

As the sun dipped below the Kansas horizon, casting long shadows across the sprawling Koch Industries headquarters, Julia Flesher Koch found herself immersed in the intricate tapestry of family history and business acumen. Chapter 2 delves into the foundations of the Koch fortune, exploring the pivotal moments that propelled the family into the upper echelons of American industry.

The narrative unfolds against the backdrop of post-World War II America, a time of economic resurgence and industrial expansion. Fred C. Koch's ingenuity and foresight in the oil and chemical industries laid the groundwork for what would become one of the largest privately-owned companies in the world. Through meticulous research and captivating storytelling, we uncover the challenges and triumphs that marked the early years of Koch Industries.

The chapter meticulously traces the family's journey through the turbulent waters of business, navigating challenges ranging from market fluctuations to family disputes. The four Koch brothers – Frederick, Charles, David, and William – emerged as a formidable force, each contributing a unique skill set to the family enterprise. The evolution of Koch Industries into a diversified conglomerate, spanning energy, chemicals, and commodities, serves as a testament to their collective vision and determination.

Interwoven with the narrative of business success is the exploration of the Koch family values. A commitment to free-market principles, limited government intervention, and a passion for innovation became the pillars upon which the Koch legacy rested. This chapter invites readers to delve into the family's ideological foundations, examining the interplay between wealth accumulation and the pursuit of a broader societal impact.

As Julia navigates the corridors of power within Koch Industries, we witness the delicate balance between tradition and progress. The family's commitment to fostering a culture of innovation and entrepreneurship is juxtaposed against the challenges of preserving a sense of heritage and continuity. The complexities of family dynamics come to the fore, as the torchbearers of the Koch legacy grapple with the expectations placed upon them.

The chapter concludes with a reflection on the lessons learned from the early years of Koch Industries, setting the stage for the next phase of the family's journey. As Julia Flesher Koch steps into the limelight, the narrative hints at the challenges and opportunities that lie ahead for the Guardians of Wealth, and the enduring legacy they are destined to shape.

4

Shifting Tides: Challenges and Transformations

As the pages of the Koch family saga turn, Chapter 3 explores the pivotal moments and transformative events that shaped the trajectory of the family legacy. Against the backdrop of a rapidly changing world, Julia Flesher Koch grapples with the evolving landscape of business, politics, and personal dynamics.

The chapter opens with a vivid portrayal of the economic upheavals and geopolitical shifts that characterized the latter half of the 20th century. The oil crises, technological revolutions, and geopolitical tensions set the stage for both unprecedented challenges and opportunities for Koch Industries. This section offers readers a front-row seat to the intricate dance between risk and reward that defines the lifeblood of the family empire.

Amidst the sweeping changes in the business environment, the narrative shifts to the family dynamics within the Koch clan. Tensions and alliances, ambitions and sacrifices — the personal stories of the Koch family members come to life. As the baton of leadership passes from one generation to the next, Julia faces the delicate task of balancing tradition with the demands of a modern era.

The emergence of Julia Flesher Koch as a prominent figure in both the family and the business adds a layer of complexity to the narrative. Her role as a guardian of the Koch legacy is scrutinized under the spotlight, and readers are invited to witness her strategic acumen, resilience, and the unique challenges she faces as a woman navigating the traditionally male-dominated corridors of power.

The chapter delves into the family's foray into philanthropy and political activism, exploring the intersection between wealth, influence, and societal impact. The Kochs' contributions to think tanks, educational initiatives, and political causes raise questions about the role of wealth in shaping public discourse and policy. This exploration invites readers to ponder the responsibilities that come with immense financial influence.

As the story unfolds, the family confronts controversies and criticisms, navigating the delicate balance between private enterprise and public scrutiny. The Koch legacy becomes a reflection of the broader debates around corporate power, environmental stewardship, and the role of billionaires in shaping the future of society.

Chapter 3 concludes with a sense of anticipation, as the Koch family faces the dawning of a new millennium. The stage is set for a continued exploration of the family's role as guardians of wealth, with Julia Flesher Koch at the helm, steering through uncharted waters with a mix of determination, resilience, and a commitment to shaping the legacy of the Guardians of Wealth.

5

The Phoenix Rises: Reinvention and Resilience

As the new millennium unfolds, Chapter 4 of "Guardians of Wealth: The Julia Flesher Koch Legacy" delves into a period of reinvention and resilience for the Koch family. Against the backdrop of a rapidly globalizing world, shifting economic landscapes, and an era defined by technological disruption, Julia Flesher Koch takes center stage in steering the family legacy through uncharted waters.

The chapter opens with the aftermath of the dot-com bubble, a period marked by economic uncertainties and the need for adaptive strategies. Koch Industries, under Julia's strategic leadership, navigates the complexities of a changing business landscape. The narrative unfolds the family's ventures into new industries, innovative technologies, and global markets, showcasing their ability to adapt and thrive in the face of adversity.

Readers are invited to explore Julia's role as a guardian of the family's wealth, not just in terms of financial assets but as a steward of the Koch legacy. Her strategic decisions, collaborations, and the foresight to diversify the family's portfolio paint a vivid picture of leadership under pressure. The chapter delves into the intricate balance between risk and prudence, innovation and tradition, as the Koch family writes a new chapter in its storied history.

Amidst the business challenges, the narrative also intertwines personal stories within the family. Julia's relationships with her children and the broader Koch clan are explored in the context of the responsibilities that come with immense wealth. The complexities of family dynamics, succession planning, and the transmission of values become central themes, offering readers a glimpse into the human side of the guardianship journey.

A significant portion of the chapter is dedicated to the Koch family's evolving approach to philanthropy. The establishment of foundations, charitable initiatives, and partnerships signal a shift in the family's focus toward social impact. Readers witness the delicate dance between private wealth and public responsibility, as the Kochs grapple with the moral and ethical dimensions of their influence on society.

The narrative also navigates the family's engagement with environmental and social issues, exploring the delicate intersection between business interests and sustainability. The Kochs' stance on climate change, corporate responsibility, and the role of private enterprise in addressing societal challenges adds layers of complexity to the family's legacy.

As the chapter draws to a close, a sense of anticipation lingers in the air. The Koch family, guided by Julia Flesher Koch's vision, stands at the precipice of a new era. The phoenix rises from the ashes of challenges, embodying the spirit of reinvention and resilience that defines the Guardians of Wealth. The stage is set for the unfolding drama of legacy and ambition to continue in the chapters that lie ahead.

6

Legacy in Flux: Navigating Generational Shifts

In the fifth chapter of "Guardians of Wealth: The Julia Flesher Koch Legacy," the narrative probes the intricate dynamics of generational transition within the Koch family. As Julia Flesher Koch grapples with the evolving landscape of both business and family, the chapter unfolds against the backdrop of generational shifts, with the spotlight on the heirs apparent and the challenges they face in upholding the family legacy.

The chapter opens with a glimpse into the emerging roles of Julia's children within Koch Industries and the family's broader enterprises. The intricate dance of mentorship, responsibility, and the expectations placed on the shoulders of the next generation sets the stage for a compelling exploration of familial ties and corporate succession. The reader witnesses the delicate balance between preserving the family ethos and embracing innovation as the torch passes from one generation to the next.

As the business landscape continues to transform, the narrative delves into the family's response to technological disruptions, global economic shifts, and the ever-changing demands of the industries in which they operate. Julia, now a seasoned matriarch, faces the challenge of aligning tradition with innovation, ensuring that the family's values endure while remaining relevant in an ever-evolving world.

The chapter explores the complexities of managing a family fortune, touching on the intricacies of estate planning, wealth preservation, and the perpetuation of the family's philanthropic endeavors. Readers are invited to witness the delicate negotiations and strategic decisions that shape the legacy, with a keen eye on the interplay between financial stewardship and societal impact.

In the realm of philanthropy, the narrative deepens the exploration of the causes and initiatives championed by the Koch family. The reader gains insights into the evolution of their social impact endeavors, examining how the family's values and priorities shift with each passing generation. Questions of corporate social responsibility, environmental sustainability, and social justice become central themes in the family's ongoing commitment to leave a positive mark on the world.

As the chapter progresses, the narrative also touches upon the external factors influencing the Koch legacy, including the broader societal perceptions of wealth, power, and corporate influence. The family's engagements with political and social issues come under scrutiny, prompting a reflection on the delicate balance between private enterprise and public responsibility.

Chapter 5 concludes with an air of anticipation, leaving the reader on the cusp of a new phase in the Koch family's journey. The legacy, now in the hands of a new generation, stands at a crossroads, poised to navigate the complexities of the modern era. The stage is set for the continued exploration of the Guardians of Wealth and the legacy they are destined to shape.

7

Crossroads of Influence: The Koch Legacy in the 21st Century

As the story unfolds in Chapter 6 of "Guardians of Wealth: The Julia Flesher Koch Legacy," the Koch family finds itself at a critical juncture, navigating the complex intersection of business, politics, and societal impact in the 21st century. Julia Flesher Koch, at the helm of the family legacy, faces unprecedented challenges and opportunities, marking a pivotal moment in the ongoing saga of the Guardians of Wealth.

The chapter opens against the backdrop of a rapidly changing global landscape. The family's businesses, now firmly entrenched in various sectors, navigate the intricacies of a digital age, artificial intelligence, and the challenges posed by an interconnected world. The narrative takes readers on a journey through the technological disruptions, economic shifts, and geopolitical uncertainties that define the contemporary era, exploring how the Koch legacy adapts to remain a powerhouse in the business world.

Julia's leadership style and strategic decisions come under the spotlight as the family steers Koch Industries through the complexities of a globalized marketplace. The chapter delves into the delicate balance between profit motives and ethical considerations, examining how the family grapples with issues of corporate responsibility, sustainability, and the evolving expectations of a socially conscious consumer base.

The political landscape becomes a focal point of exploration, with the Koch family's influence in policy and advocacy coming to the forefront. Readers witness the family's engagements with political causes, the shaping of public discourse, and the complexities of balancing personal ideologies with corporate interests. The interplay between wealth, power, and political influence takes center stage, inviting readers to reflect on the role of private entities in shaping the future of nations.

Amidst the challenges, the chapter also unravels the personal stories within the Koch family. Relationships, conflicts, and the intricate dance of familial bonds come to life as Julia navigates the complexities of being both a matriarch and a business leader. The reader is invited to witness the human side of the Guardians of Wealth, exploring the personal sacrifices, triumphs, and challenges that accompany the stewardship of a vast family fortune.

The philanthropic endeavors of the Koch family deepen in significance, with a focus on addressing pressing global issues. The narrative explores how the family's values manifest in their social impact initiatives, from education and healthcare to environmental conservation and beyond. The reader is prompted to consider the role of immense wealth in contributing to positive change on a societal scale.

As Chapter 6 draws to a close, a sense of anticipation lingers in the air. The Koch legacy, now firmly anchored in the 21st century, stands at the crossroads of influence, facing the dual challenge of preserving tradition while adapting to the demands of a rapidly evolving world. The Guardians of Wealth prepare to script the next chapter in their legacy, leaving readers eager to uncover the twists and turns that lie ahead.

8

Echoes of the Past, Visions of the Future

In the seventh chapter of "Guardians of Wealth: The Julia Flesher Koch Legacy," the narrative deepens, exploring the interplay of history, foresight, and the enduring legacy of the Koch family. Against the canvas of time, Julia Flesher Koch grapples with the echoes of the past and envisions the future, navigating a path that intertwines tradition with innovation.

The chapter opens with a reflective exploration of the family's historical footprint, tracing the lineage of values, principles, and business acumen that have transcended generations. Julia, as the torchbearer of this rich legacy, finds herself at the intersection of honoring tradition and steering the family toward new horizons. The narrative takes readers on a journey through the annals of Koch Industries, exploring the pivotal moments that shaped the family's identity.

As the family businesses continue to evolve, the chapter delves into the strategic decisions and visionary leadership that define Julia's tenure. The complexities of managing a vast empire come to life, with a keen focus on the delicate balance between risk and stability, innovation and tradition. Readers witness the ongoing saga of Koch Industries as it adapts to emerging technologies, global dynamics, and the ever-shifting currents of the business landscape.

The familial bonds within the Koch clan take center stage, as the narrative explores the relationships between Julia, her children, and the broader family network. Personal stories, conflicts, and triumphs offer a window into the human side of wealth stewardship. The challenges of succession planning, the transmission of values, and the delicate dance of managing familial expectations become central themes in this exploration of the Koch legacy.

The chapter widens its lens to scrutinize the family's philanthropic endeavors. Readers gain insight into the impact of the Koch family's charitable initiatives on education, healthcare, and societal well-being. The narrative prompts reflection on the responsibilities that come with immense wealth, exploring how the family leverages its resources to address pressing global challenges while staying true to its values.

The political landscape remains a key arena of exploration, with the family's influence in policy and advocacy continuing to shape the broader socio-political narrative. The interplay between private enterprise, political engagement, and the family's commitment to certain ideologies becomes a focal point, raising questions about the role of wealth in shaping the contours of society.

As the chapter progresses, the narrative becomes a tapestry of past, present, and future. The reader is left with a sense of anticipation, wondering how the Koch legacy will continue to unfold. Julia Flesher Koch, as the steward of this enduring dynasty, stands poised to guide the family through the complexities of the 21st century, balancing the echoes of the past with the visions of the future. The Guardians of Wealth prepare to script the next chapter, leaving readers eager to discover the twists and turns that lie ahead in this captivating family saga.

9

The Legacy Unfolds: Charting New Horizons

In the eighth chapter of "Guardians of Wealth: The Julia Flesher Koch Legacy," the narrative reaches a crescendo as the legacy of the Koch family unfolds in unexpected ways. Against a backdrop of shifting paradigms, emerging challenges, and transformative opportunities, Julia Flesher Koch navigates uncharted territory, guiding the family's destiny with a blend of resilience and strategic foresight.

The chapter opens with a reflection on the enduring values that have anchored the Koch legacy throughout its storied history. As the family grapples with societal changes, economic uncertainties, and the evolution of business models, Julia becomes a central figure in shaping the narrative of continuity and adaptation. Readers are invited to witness the delicate dance of tradition and innovation, exploring how the family's enduring principles remain a compass in the face of change.

The business landscape takes on new dimensions as Koch Industries continues to diversify, embracing emerging technologies and global opportunities.

The narrative delves into the strategic decisions that propel the family's enterprises forward, examining how the Guardians of Wealth navigate the challenges posed by a dynamic and interconnected world. Themes of sustainability, ethical business practices, and corporate responsibility come to the forefront, echoing the family's commitment to leaving a positive impact on the planet.

Family dynamics take a nuanced turn as the next generation assumes more prominent roles within the family enterprise. The chapter explores the interplay of generational perspectives, the transmission of values, and the evolving responsibilities of the heirs apparent. Julia grapples with the delicate task of ensuring a smooth transition of leadership while fostering a culture of innovation and adaptability.

The philanthropic arm of the Koch legacy undergoes further evolution, with a focus on addressing pressing global issues. The family's commitment to social impact initiatives gains new dimensions, reflecting the changing needs of society. Readers witness how the family deploys its wealth not only to sustain their legacy but also to make meaningful contributions to the betterment of humanity, exploring avenues that align with their values and societal priorities.

Political engagement remains a defining feature of the family's legacy, with the Kochs continuing to wield influence in shaping public discourse and policy. The chapter unfolds the family's stance on contemporary political issues, sparking reflections on the intersection of wealth, power, and the responsibilities that come with political influence.

As the narrative reaches its climax, readers are left with a sense of awe and anticipation. The legacy of the Koch family, now firmly embedded in the fabric of American history, stands at the forefront of wealth stewardship and societal impact. Julia Flesher Koch, with her resilience, foresight, and commitment to the family's values, emerges as a pivotal figure in the ongoing saga of the Guardians of Wealth. The stage is set for the legacy to unfold in new and unforeseen ways, leaving readers eager to discover the unwritten chapters that lie ahead.

10

Reckoning and Renewal: The Legacy's Epiphany

As "Guardians of Wealth: The Julia Flesher Koch Legacy" enters its penultimate chapter, the narrative takes a contemplative turn. Chapter 9, titled "Reckoning and Renewal," unravels against a backdrop of profound self-reflection, societal reckoning, and the family's response to the winds of change.

The chapter opens with the family confronting reckonings from within and without. The Koch legacy, now spanning decades, faces scrutiny on various fronts – ethical considerations, the impact of business practices, and the role of wealth in shaping societal narratives. Julia Flesher Koch, at the forefront of this introspective journey, grapples with the complexities of balancing tradition with a rapidly evolving global consciousness.

The narrative delves into the challenges posed by changing social expectations and a heightened awareness of environmental, social, and governance (ESG) considerations. The family's response to calls for increased transparency, ethical business practices, and a heightened commitment to sustainability becomes a central theme. Readers witness a family in transition, embracing the opportunity for renewal and recalibration in the face of contemporary challenges.

Business dynamics take center stage as Koch Industries navigates the imperatives of a new era. The chapter explores the family's response to technological disruptions, shifting consumer preferences, and the imperative for corporate responsibility. Themes of innovation, adaptability, and a renewed commitment to ethical practices shape the narrative of the legacy's evolution.

The familial landscape undergoes a transformative phase as Julia, alongside the next generation, reflects on the future of the family legacy. Succession planning, the transmission of values, and fostering a culture of inclusivity become pivotal considerations. The narrative invites readers to witness the family's journey through introspection and adaptation, navigating the complexities of generational transitions.

Philanthropy becomes a conduit for renewal as the family redirects its charitable initiatives to address contemporary societal challenges. The legacy's impact on education, healthcare, and environmental causes takes on a renewed sense of purpose, aligning with the family's commitment to positive societal change.

Political engagement, a hallmark of the Koch legacy, undergoes a nuanced transformation. The family grapples with its role in shaping political landscapes, reevaluating strategies in light of evolving socio-political dynamics. The chapter unfolds the family's endeavors to contribute meaningfully to public discourse, navigating the fine line between influence and responsibility.

As Chapter 9 reaches its zenith, readers find themselves at a juncture of anticipation and reflection. The Koch legacy, having weathered reckonings and embraced renewal, stands poised on the brink of a new era. Julia Flesher

Koch emerges as a steward not only of wealth but of the family's commitment to ethical leadership, societal impact, and a legacy that resonates with the values of a changing world. The concluding chapter beckons, promising a culmination of the Guardians of Wealth saga and a glimpse into the future that awaits the Koch legacy.

11

Beyond Boundaries: A Legacy in Full Bloom

In the final chapter of "Guardians of Wealth: The Julia Flesher Koch Legacy," the narrative converges on the culmination of the Koch family saga. Titled "Beyond Boundaries: A Legacy in Full Bloom," this chapter explores the enduring impact of the family's journey, the evolution of wealth stewardship, and the legacy that transcends generations.

The chapter opens with a panoramic view of the Koch legacy, shaped by the visionary leadership of Julia Flesher Koch. Readers witness the legacy in full bloom, a testament to the family's ability to adapt, innovate, and contribute meaningfully to the world. Against the canvas of time, the narrative unfolds the final acts of the Guardians of Wealth, encapsulating the family's enduring values and the indelible mark they've left on the realms of business, philanthropy, and societal change.

The business empire, rooted in the lessons of the past and propelled by the vision of the present, stands as a symbol of resilience and adaptability. The chapter navigates the family's ventures into emerging industries, technological landscapes, and global markets, showcasing their ability to not only survive but thrive in an ever-changing world.

Familial bonds and generational transitions take center stage as the narrative explores how the legacy is passed on to the next stewards. Themes of mentorship, shared values, and the delicate dance of tradition and progress become focal points, inviting readers to witness the continuity of the family ethos across time.

Philanthropy becomes a hallmark of the legacy's impact, with the family's charitable initiatives leaving an indelible mark on education, healthcare, environmental conservation, and societal well-being. The chapter delves into the family's commitment to making a positive difference in the world, highlighting the interconnectedness between immense wealth and a responsibility to contribute to the betterment of humanity.

Political engagement, though nuanced, remains a part of the legacy's tapestry. The chapter explores how the family continues to navigate the intersection of wealth and influence, shaping public discourse, and contributing to the development of policies that align with their values.

As the legacy unfolds, the narrative takes moments to reflect on the personal stories within the Koch family. Readers witness the triumphs, challenges, and the human side of wealth stewardship. Julia Flesher Koch, as the matriarch who steered the family through decades of change, emerges as a central figure in this epic tale of success, resilience, and impact.

The chapter concludes with a reflection on the legacy's ripple effect. Beyond financial wealth, the family's imprint on societal narratives, business practices, and philanthropic endeavors becomes a lasting testament to the Guardians of Wealth. The reader is left with a sense of fulfillment, having journeyed through the highs and lows of a family legacy that transcends the boundaries of time.

As the final pages turn, the legacy of the Koch family stands as a beacon of inspiration and a model of responsible wealth stewardship. The story of the Guardians of Wealth concludes, leaving a legacy in full bloom and inviting readers to ponder the profound impact that immense wealth can have on shaping the course of history.

12

Reflections and Continuity: The Legacy Lives On

In this concluding chapter of "Guardians of Wealth: The Julia Flesher Koch Legacy," the narrative takes a moment for reflection, acknowledging the profound impact of the Koch family journey and contemplating the continuity of the legacy into the future.

The chapter opens with a reflective gaze upon the entire narrative, inviting readers to journey back through the chapters, tracing the evolution of the Koch legacy. As the tale of the Guardians of Wealth unfolds, the narrative pauses to consider the enduring values, pivotal moments, and the collective wisdom that shaped the family's trajectory.

The theme of continuity becomes central as the narrative explores how the legacy lives on through the next generations. The torchbearers of the family ethos, informed by the experiences and lessons of their predecessors, step into leadership roles with a commitment to preserving the legacy's core values while embracing the imperatives of a new era.

Readers are granted a glimpse into the family's evolving role in societal narratives. The chapter examines how the Koch legacy, beyond its financial impact, contributes to shaping conversations around wealth, responsibility, and the role of influential families in the broader context of society. Themes of transparency, ethical stewardship, and the intersection of wealth and social impact resonate as the legacy continues to unfold.

Philanthropy takes on a renewed significance in this chapter, with the family's charitable initiatives adapting to the evolving needs of the world. The legacy's imprint on education, healthcare, and environmental causes becomes a focal point, demonstrating a commitment to positive societal change that endures across generations.

As the narrative explores the family's place in the ever-shifting landscape of politics, readers witness how the Koch legacy navigates the complexities of influence, responsibility, and engagement. The family's stance on political issues reflects an ongoing commitment to contributing meaningfully to public discourse and shaping policies that align with their values.

The concluding chapter also pays tribute to Julia Flesher Koch, the matriarch whose leadership and vision steered the family through the various chapters of their journey. Her resilience, strategic acumen, and commitment to the family's values become a timeless example of effective wealth stewardship.

The final pages of the book invite readers to contemplate the broader implications of the Koch legacy. How does immense wealth influence the course of history? What responsibilities come with financial abundance, and how can a family legacy contribute positively to the world? The legacy of the Guardians of Wealth becomes not just a story but a canvas upon which readers can project their own thoughts about the role of wealth in society.

As the book concludes, the legacy of the Koch family remains a living testament to the intricate dance between wealth, power, responsibility, and the indomitable spirit of those who shape the course of history. The story may have reached its final chapter, but the echoes of the Koch legacy resonate, inviting readers to carry the narrative forward, pondering the profound implications of wealth stewardship in the ongoing tapestry of human history.

13

Epilogue: A Lasting Legacy

As we conclude the narrative of "Guardians of Wealth: The Julia Flesher Koch Legacy," this epilogue offers a final reflection on the enduring legacy of the Koch family. Beyond the pages of this book, the impact of the Guardians of Wealth resonates across time, leaving an indelible mark on the intersection of business, wealth, and societal influence.

The epilogue begins by revisiting key moments in the family's journey, emphasizing the pivotal decisions, transformative periods, and the resilience that defined the Koch legacy. Readers are encouraged to reflect on the lessons learned from the family's experiences, both triumphs, and challenges, as they navigated the intricate dance of wealth stewardship.

A central theme of the epilogue is the continuity of the legacy. The narrative explores how the values instilled by Julia Flesher Koch and her predecessors continue to shape the family's trajectory. The next generations, poised to carry the torch forward, become custodians of not only financial wealth but a rich tapestry of principles, ethics, and a commitment to societal betterment.

Philanthropy, an integral part of the Koch legacy, comes under the spotlight in the epilogue. The narrative contemplates the ongoing impact of the family's charitable initiatives, questioning how the legacy's contributions resonate in a world grappling with social, environmental, and economic challenges. Themes of education, healthcare, and sustainability continue to be pillars of the family's philanthropic endeavors.

The epilogue also explores the family's evolving role in public narratives. How does the Koch legacy influence discussions around wealth, business ethics, and the responsibilities of influential families? The chapter encourages readers to consider the broader implications of wealth and the multifaceted nature of the family's impact on societal conversations.

As the narrative concludes, the epilogue contemplates the significance of the Koch legacy in the broader context of contemporary history. How will the family be remembered? What lessons does their story offer to future generations of wealth stewards? The epilogue invites readers to ponder these questions, recognizing that the Guardians of Wealth have played a unique role in shaping the narrative of wealth, power, and societal responsibility.

In the final paragraphs, the epilogue leaves readers with a sense of closure and continuity. The Koch legacy, having weathered the tides of time, stands as a testament to the intricate interplay of wealth, values, and the enduring spirit of those who bear the mantle of financial guardianship.

As the book concludes, readers are invited to carry the narrative forward in their minds, contemplating the profound implications of wealth stewardship and the legacy that extends beyond the confines of the pages. The story of the Koch family becomes not just a historical account but a living reflection on the complexities and responsibilities of wealth in the ongoing saga of human civilization.

14

Summary

"Guardians of Wealth: The Julia Flesher Koch Legacy" is a multifaceted narrative that unfolds across twelve chapters, exploring the intricate tapestry of the Koch family's journey through wealth, business, and societal impact. At its core, the story revolves around Julia Flesher Koch, the matriarch who becomes a central figure in steering the family legacy through decades of change.

The narrative begins by delving into the origins of the Koch family, tracing their ascent from humble beginnings to the establishment of Koch Industries, a conglomerate that spans various industries. The story unfolds against the backdrop of a changing America, intertwining the family's business successes with the values and principles that define their approach to wealth.

Throughout the chapters, the narrative navigates key moments in the family's history, exploring the challenges and triumphs that shaped the Koch legacy. Themes of business innovation, familial dynamics, philanthropy, and political engagement are interwoven, providing readers with a comprehensive understanding of the multifaceted nature of wealth stewardship.

As Julia Flesher Koch takes on the role of the family's matriarch, the narrative deepens, offering insights into her personal journey, leadership style, and the challenges she faces in balancing tradition with the demands of a modern era. The legacy's evolution unfolds, encompassing generational shifts, societal reckonings, and a renewed commitment to philanthropy and social impact.

In the final chapters, the narrative explores the legacy's enduring impact and the family's reflections on their journey. Themes of continuity, generational transition, and the intersection of wealth and responsibility come to the forefront, inviting readers to reflect on the broader implications of the Koch legacy in the context of contemporary history.

The book concludes with an epilogue that offers a final reflection on the lasting legacy of the Koch family. The epilogue contemplates the family's ongoing role in societal narratives, the continuity of their values, and the multifaceted nature of their impact on wealth stewardship. The narrative encourages readers to carry the story forward, pondering the profound implications of wealth in the ongoing tapestry of human civilization.

www.ingramcontent.com/pod-product-compliance
Lightning Source LLC
LaVergne TN
LVHW010442070526
838199LV00066B/6150